岸本斉史

When the time came to put together the plot for *Naruto* volume 53, I consulted my wife, and this is what resulted. Stories about Mother.

—Masashi Kishimoto, 2010

Author/artist Masashi Kishimoto was born in 1974 in rural Okayama Prefecture, Japan. After spending time in art college, he won the Hop Step Award for new manga artists with his manga **Karakuri** (Mechanism). Kishimoto decided to base his next story on traditional Japanese culture. His first version of **Naruto**, drawn in 1997, was a one-shot story about fox spirits; his final version, which debuted in **Weekly Shonen Jump** in 1999, quickly became the most popular ninja manga in Japan.

NARUTO VOL. 53
SHONEN JUMP Manga Edition
This graphic novel contains material that was originally published in English in SHONEN JUMP #98–101. Artwork in the magazine may have been slightly altered from that presented here.

STORY AND ART BY MASASHI KISHIMOTO

Translation/Mari Morimoto
Touch-up Art & Lettering/Inori Fukuda Trant, Sabrina Heep
Design/Sam Elzway
Series Editor/Joel Enos
Graphic Novel Editor/Megan Bates

Printed in the U.S.A.

Published by VIZ Media, LLC
P.O. Box 77010
San Francisco, CA 94107

10 9 8 7 6 5 4 3 2 1
First printing, December 2011

NARUTO

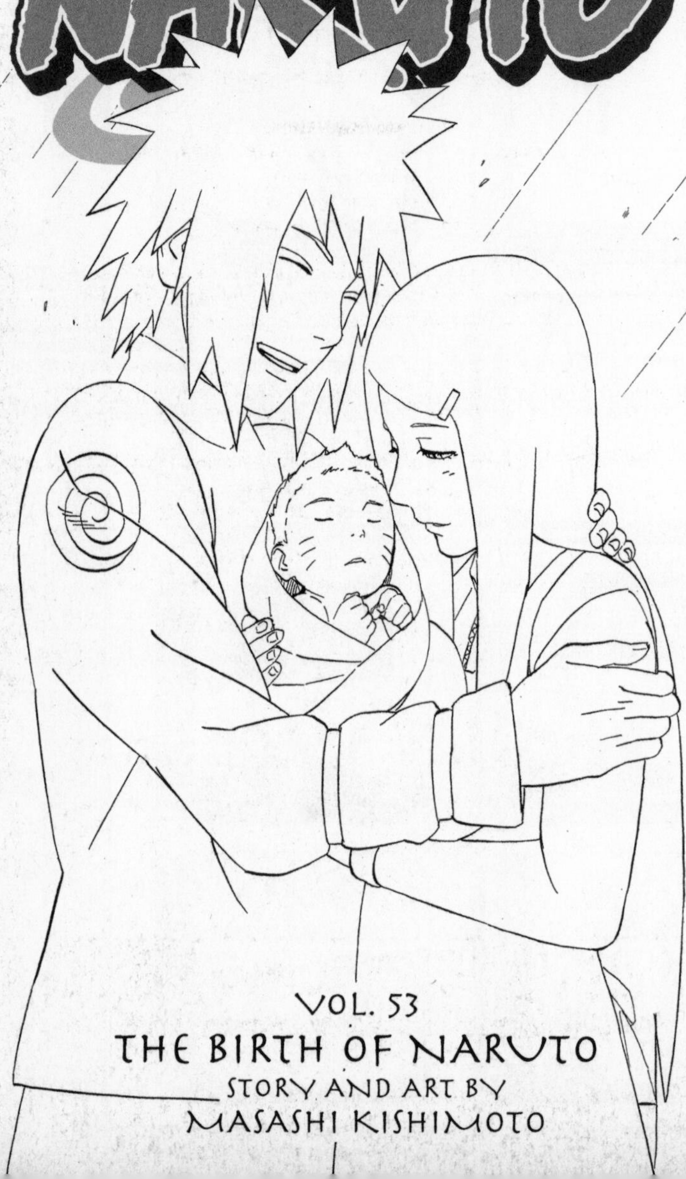

VOL. 53
THE BIRTH OF NARUTO

STORY AND ART BY
MASASHI KISHIMOTO

CHARACTERS

Naruto ナルト

Sasuke サスケ

Kakashi カカシ

Sakura サクラ

Sai サイ

Yamato ヤマト

Tsunade 綱手

Jiraiya 自来也

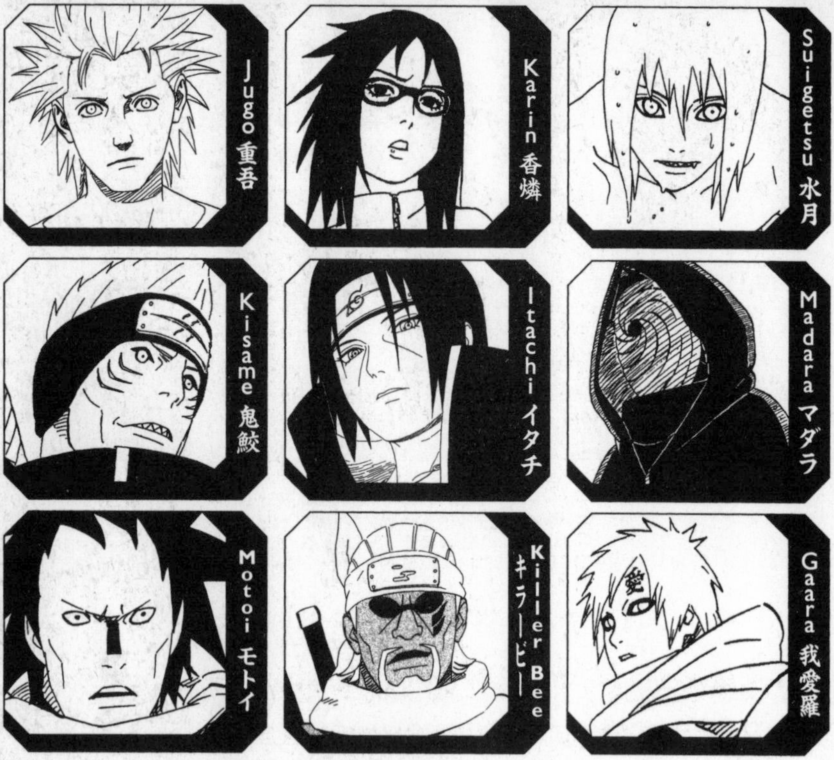

THE STORY SO FAR...

Naruto, the biggest troublemaker at the Ninja Academy in the Village of Konohagakure, finally becomes a ninja along with his classmates Sasuke and Sakura. They grow and mature through countless trials and battles. However, Sasuke, unable to give up his quest for vengeance, leaves Konohagakure to seek Orochimaru and his power…

In the years that pass, Naruto engages in fierce battles against the Tailed Beast-targeting Akatsuki. Elsewhere, after winning the heroic battle against Itachi and learning his older brother's true intentions, Sasuke allies with the Akatsuki and sets out to destroy Konoha.

Upon Madara's declaration of war, an Allied Shinobi Force is formed. Naruto, sent away in the name of protecting the jinchûriki, begins training to control Nine Tails. As he struggles, he learns of Bee and Motoi's past, and realizes the importance of trust!!

NARUTO

VOL. 53

THE BIRTH OF NARUTO

CONTENTS

Number 495: Dark Naruto, Defeated!!

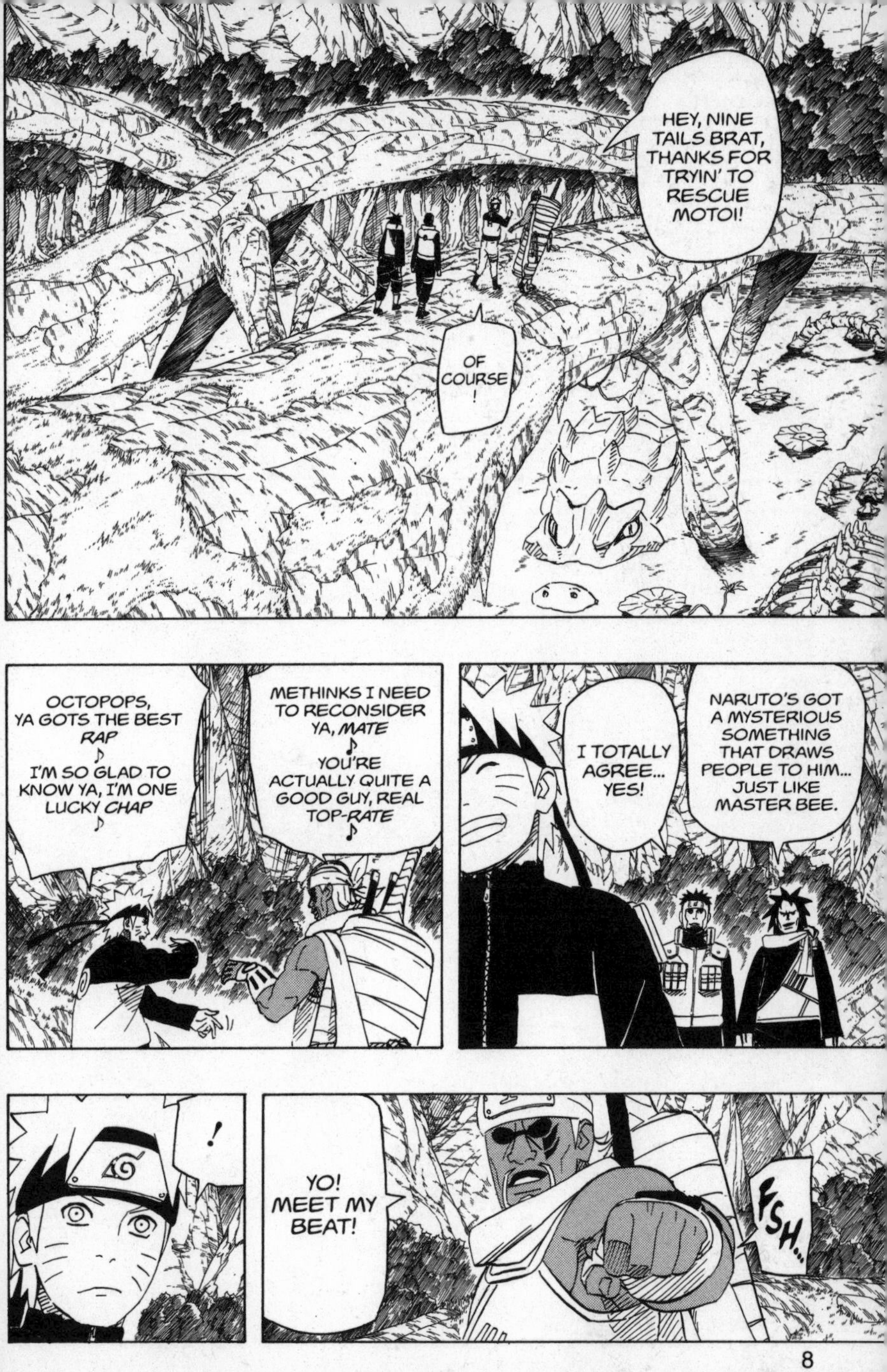
HEY, NINE TAILS BRAT, THANKS FOR TRYIN' TO RESCUE MOTOI!
OF COURSE!
OCTOPOPS, YA GOTS THE BEST RAP ♪ I'M SO GLAD TO KNOW YA, I'M ONE LUCKY CHAP ♪
METHINKS I NEED TO RECONSIDER YA, MATE ♪ YOU'RE ACTUALLY QUITE A GOOD GUY, REAL TOP-RATE ♪
NARUTO'S GOT A MYSTERIOUS SOMETHING THAT DRAWS PEOPLE TO HIM... JUST LIKE MASTER BEE.
I TOTALLY AGREE... YES!
YO! MEET MY BEAT!
FSH...
!

READ THIS WAY

SHADDUP, YA KNOW ♪
...!

READ THIS WAY

HAVEN'T YOU LEARNED YOUR LESSON YET? IT'LL BE THE SAME, NO MATTER HOW MANY TIMES WE GO AT IT.
YOU CANNOT DEFEAT ME...
THD-THD-THD-
YEAH...
I CAN'T DEFEAT YOU BY FORCE...
WE USE THE EXACT SAME MOVES.
YOU CAN'T CHASE ME OUT.
I KNOW YOU BETTER THAN YOU KNOW YOURSELF.
THEN... YOU ALREADY KNOW?
SSH...
...
KNOW WHAT?!

READ THIS WAY

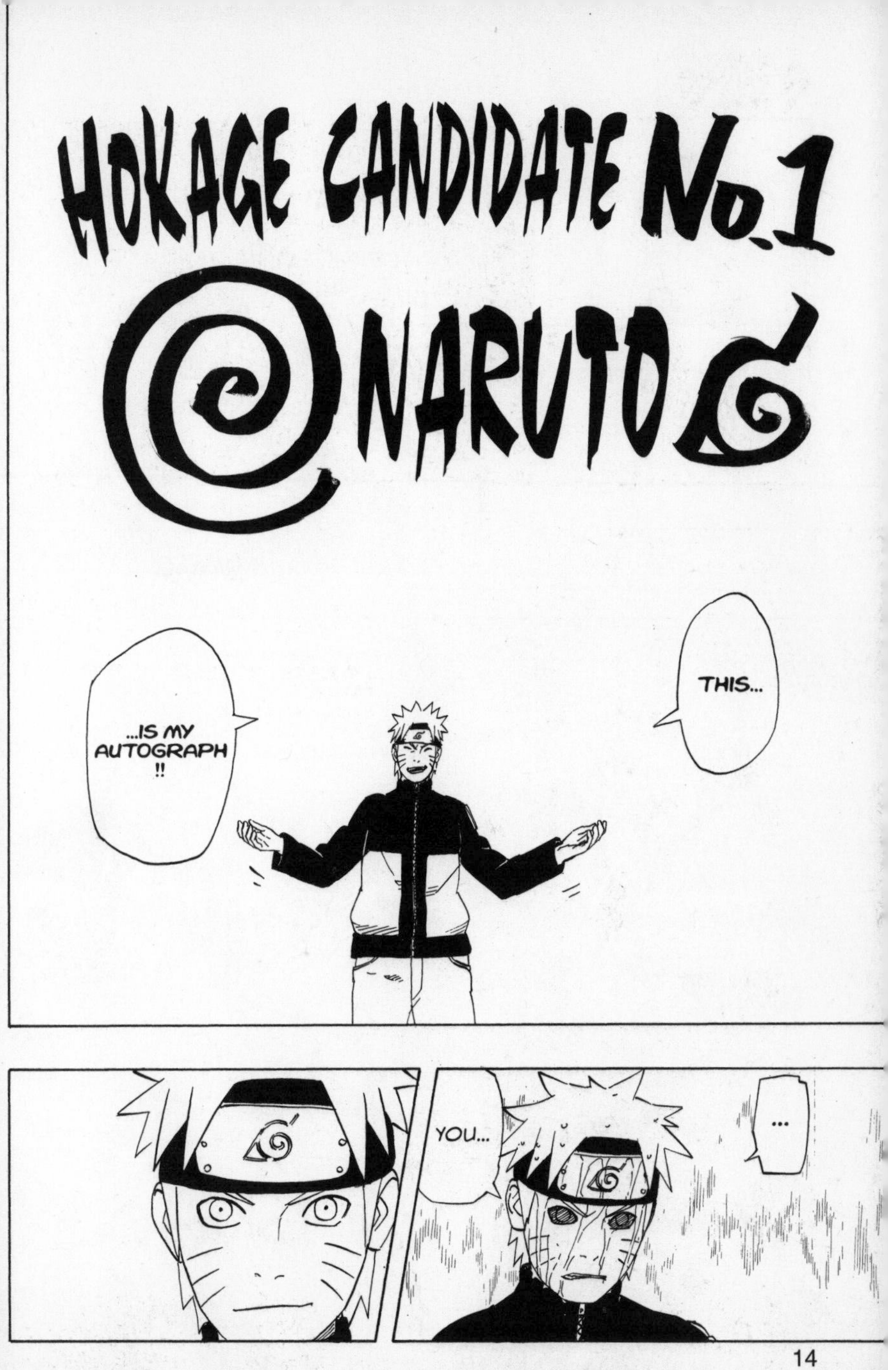
HOKAGE CANDIDATE No.1
NARUTO
THIS...
...IS MY AUTOGRAPH !!
...
YOU...

READ THIS WAY

I NEED TO BELIEVE IN MYSELF!
I NEED TO TRUST THE *ME* THAT THE VILLAGERS BELIEVE IN.
...
...
UNH...
UNH... UNH...

READ THIS WAY

YOU NEED TO BE ME!
SINCE YOU ARE ME.
CHAK
?!
THANKS FOR EVERYTHING...
BUT IT'S ALL RIGHT NOW.

READ THIS WAY

HEH HEH...!
...
IT WENT WELL, I TAKE IT?
TOO EARLY TO CELE-BRATE...
FOOL, YA FOOL!
!
SPLISH
SPLISH

FROM THIS MOMENT... I SHALL BE YOUR *INSTRUCTOR* ♪ YA BETTER PREPARE YOURSELF, OR ELSE YA MAY SUFFER DEATH OR *TORTURE* ♪
SHALL WE TRY CONTROLLING NINE TAILS' POWER NOW?!
SHUP
BRING IT ON!!
FOLLOW ME, NARUTO!
TAK

UH... AM I COMING TOO?
SURE!
MOTOI ?
I MUST MAKE MY PERIODIC REPORT TO KUMOGAKURE, SO NO...
THANK YOU FOR YOUR HELP.
WELL, IT'S PROBABLY NOT GOING TO BE ANY EASIER FROM HERE ON OUT.
W- WHOA...!

SWOOOSH
THERE'S SOMETHING ON THE OTHER SIDE...?
SWOOOOSH
!
SWOO
YOU'LL BE FIGHTING NINE TAILS HERE!!

Number 496: Reunion with Nine Tails!!

NO NO! THOSE STONE STATUES WERE CARVED WITHOUT HEADS...
...FOR A REASON.
HOW AM I SUPPOSED TO FIGHT NINE TAILS HERE?!
HOW DO I EVEN FACE HIM?!
FIGHT NINE TAILS?! NO WAY... HE DOESN'T HAVE TO DO ANYTHING EXCESSIVE, DOES HE?!
DO YA REALLY THINK YA CAN ACHIEVE BIJU CONTROL WITHOUT BEING EXCESSIVE, FOOL, YA FOOL!
THIS IS A SACRED PLACE WHERE THOSE SELECTED AS JINCHŪRIKI HAVE LONG COME TO UNDERGO PURIFICATION CEREMONIES.

READ THIS WAY

ULP
I'M THE TRUE YOU...
NARUTO, USE A SHADOW DOPPEL-GANGER.
THE RISKS ARE TOO HIGH.
THIS IS A SACRED PLACE, FOOL, YA FOOL!
MANY GENER-ATIONS OF KUMOGAKURE ANCESTORS WATCH OVER THIS PLACE... SUCH TRICKS WON'T WORK!!
BUT...!
COMMANDER YAMATO! I CAME HERE TO GAIN CONTROL OVER THE NINE TAILS' POWER!
I HAVE TO DO THIS. I'M NOT RUNNING AWAY!
...I HAVE TO BELIEVE IN MYSELF!!
FSH
REE
EE...

READ THIS WAY

POP!
KIDDING!!
THERE WAS JUST A SWITCH IN THERE.
...
A-HA HA HA HA
I HADDA DO IT!
I PLAYED THAT TRICK MY FIRST TIME, *TOO* ♪ THOSE HEADLESS STATUES ARE JUST BROKEN TO SCARE A *FOOL* ♪
IRK
I THOUGHT THIS WAS A SACRED PLACE!! FOOLS, YA FOOLS!!
!
!
RRRRUMBLE...
...
I-IS THIS...?

YA NEED TO GO IN THERE, SIT DOWN, CLOSE YOUR EYES AND FOCUS...
...JUST LIKE AT THE WATERFALL.
AND THEN YOU'LL MEET UP WITH YOUR BIJU.
SHF
I ONCE KNEW A DRILL THAT LET ME SEE NINE TAILS INSIDE MY HEART...
ALL JINCHÛRIKI CAN DO THAT... THIS IS A LITTLE DIFFERENT, OKAY?!
LISTEN CLOSELY TO MY TALE! ♪
NARUTO... WHAT WAS USED TO SEAL IN THE NINE TAIL? ♪
HUH?
A TETRAGRAM SEAL.
A TETRAGRAM SEAL, EH... VERY IMPRESSIVE.
A LOT MORE SOLID THAN MY OWN TEKKÔFÛIN STEEL SHELL SEAL...
...YA GOTS THE KEY ON YA?
...YUP!
FWA
WAFT
WAFT

SO... YOU DO HAVE TO UNDO THE SEAL...
WHAT IF... HE'S NOT ABLE TO CONTROL HIM...
...AND NINE TAILS FULLY MANIFESTS, WHAT THEN?!
WE'LL SEAL HIM AWAY IN THIS PLACE!
THAT'S WHAT THIS PLACE IS FOR, AS WELL.
WE'D TRAP NINE TAILS HERE UNTIL WE GET A NEW HOST ♪
THOUGH THAT'D BE A WORSE OUTCOME THAN MOST ♪
BUT...
THAT WON'T HAPPEN ...!
I SWEAR I'LL SUCCEED!

READ THIS WAY

封
...
YO...
SPOOKY GLARE, AS USUAL.
...
NARUTO... YOU...
WHAT'S UP?
WAFT...
WHERE'D THE REAL YOU GO?
I DON'T SENSE HIM...!

READ THIS WAY
YOU MAY HAVE CONQUERED YOUR HATRED... DON'T LET YOUR GUARD GET HAZY ♪
封
I'M RIGHT HERE... RIGHT IN FRONT OF YOUR EYES!
FSH
NINE TAILS IS A LUMP OF LOATHING... AND SOMEWHAT CRAZY ♪
FRIP
封
WUP
!?
WHAT ARE YOU PLOTTING?
WHUF
TUG
CAN'T YA SEE MY MOUTH IS FULL?
YOINK

FWP
BOF
BOF
BOF
BOF
BOF
SWOOO...
WUMP
UGH!
SQUIRK
KLUNK
WHRRR...
KLAK
KLAK

READ THIS WAY

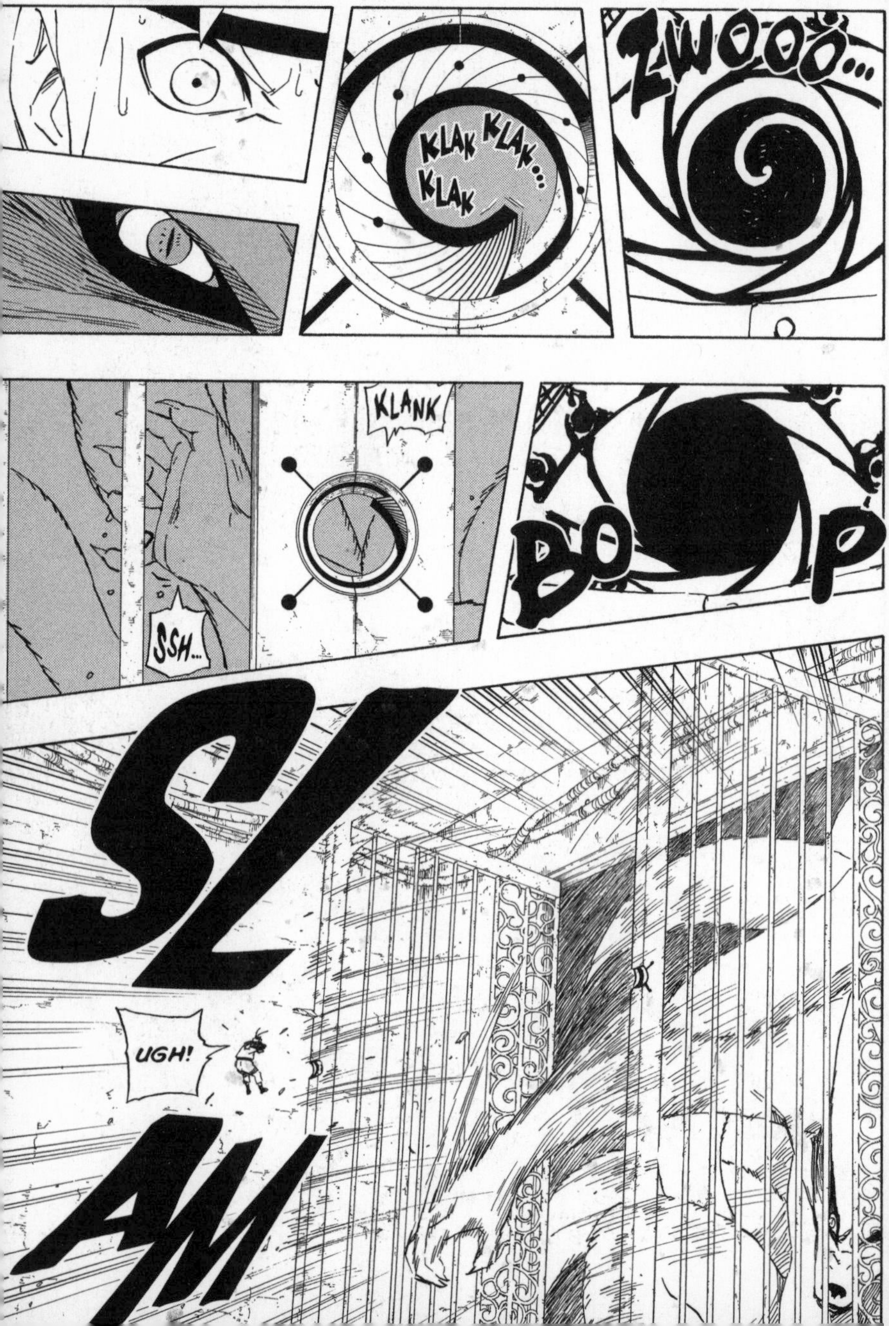

WHEN NINE TAILS EMERGES...
WUF
...GRAB NINE TAILS' CHAKRA AND PULL HARD!!
ZWOOOO...

CHAKRA CAN ONLY BE CAPTURED USING CHAKRA... THAT'S HOW IT GOES ♪
SO STEAL NINE TAILS' CHAKRA DIRECTLY FROM NINE TAILS... FROM RIGHT UNDER HIS NOSE ♪
BUMP
RAAAAAAWR!!!
!!
KRAK
GRRR...
WHOOSH
CHONK
WHOOOOOSH

YA NEED TO TOUCH NINE TAILS DIRECTLY AND STICK YOUR CHAKRA ONTO NINE TAILS'. ONLY THEN CAN YA PULL ON IT.
IT'S GONNA BE LIKE A TUG-OF-WAR GOT IT?!
RRR...
GRRRRR!!
RRRRRR
RRRRRRRR
ZWOOO...
RAAAAAWR!!!
THUCK
THUCK
THUCK
THUCK
GAH...

READ THIS WAY

NARUTO

Number 497: Nine Tails vs. Naruto!!

DON'T MOCK ME...

THANKS, OCTO-POPS!!
NRRR?
GRRR

FIZZZ
PSSH...
FWP
FWOOOOO
WHAM
ZWOOO
ZWP
BOOOF

READ THIS WAY

THUNK
SWISH
!
RAWWR !!
WAH!!
TAK
ZAP

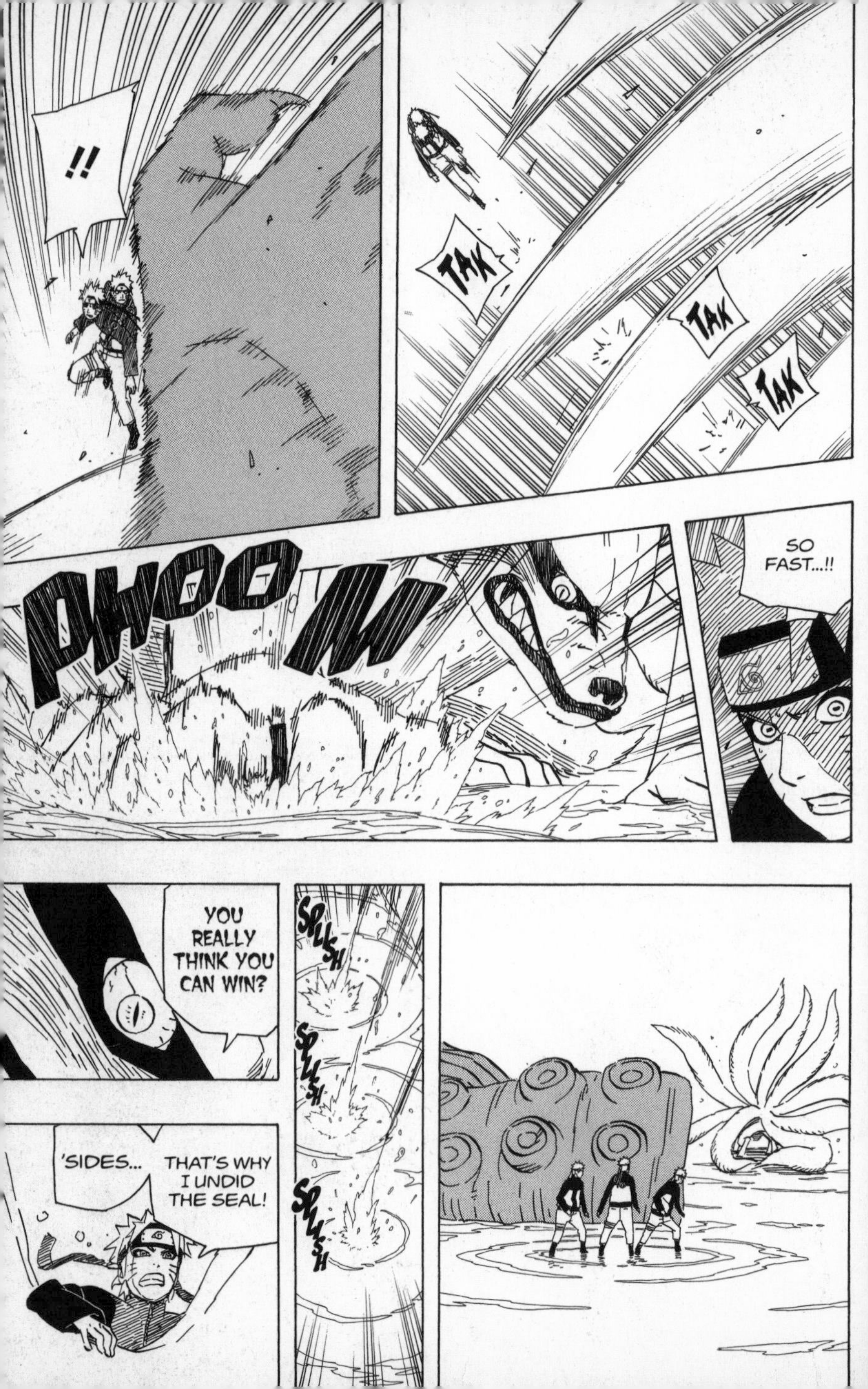

TAK
TAK
TAK
!!
SO FAST...!!
PHOOM
YOU REALLY THINK YOU CAN WIN?
SPLSH
SPLSH
SPLSH
THAT'S WHY I UNDID THE SEAL!
'SIDES...

CLAMP
SPLASH
GOTCHA!
...
BOOF
HURL
YAAAAAAH!!
WUMP
!!

SLAM
SWISH
!!
TAKE THIS!!
VOOM
SH

WIND STYLE! RASEN-SHURIKEN!!
ARGH!

NOW!
CLENCH
ZWEE...
BOOF
THD-
UGGH...!
BOOF
THD-THD-THD-THD
ZWEE...
RRRRRRRRRRRRRRR
HE HE HEH
SKUF...
SLOSH

PWOSH!!!
UNHF...
GUH!
CLOP...
DRIBBLE
SPLASH
SLUMP...
!
HE'S WEAK! I HAVE TO...!!
UNH

READ THIS WAY

HELP...!
WHY?!
IF IT JUST WEREN'T FOR HIM!
I'LL GET REVENGE...!!
I'M SICK AND TIRED OF IT ALL!!
IT'S NOT GOING TO WORK, ANYWAY...
ALWAYS HIM...!

READ THIS WAY

YOU'LL NEVER BE ABLE TO CONTROL MY POWER!
YOU'RE JUST A WEE LITTLE PIECE OF MY HATRED!
THAT'S HIM...
BEGONE ...!
HUF
HUF
YOU'LL NEVER HAVE THE RESPECT YOU DESIRE.
SWW...
GET OUT!!
GET LOST!!
SHAD-DUP!!
SWW...
NINE TAILS' HATRED IS GREATER THAN I IMAGINED!!
THIS IS BAD FOR REAL! QUITE THE ORDEAL!!
I'LL STOP HIM!!
FSH
BLp
URK!!
BLp

READ THIS WAY

NARUTO

Number 498:
My Ma's Red Hair
...
HUH? WHERE'D YOU COME FROM?!
AND HOW COME YOU KNOW MY NAME?!
AAH... OF COURSE...
WELL THEN... WHY DON'T YOU GUESS WHO I AM, NARUTO?
...
...
TEE HEE...
DON'T TELL ME...!
YOU GOT IT?

YOU! YOU'RE NINE TAILS' TRUE FORM!!
A-HA HA HA HA!
GWA-HA HA HA HA!
THAT'S A SCARY LAUGH!!
TRYING TO TRICK ME BY TAKING THAT FORM?
YOU'RE WRONG, YA KNOW?!!
WHA
OWW ...!!
...!
...YA KNOW...?

READ THIS WAY

!
UN
F...
...
SHF...

READ THIS WAY

THERE'S SO MUCH I WANT TO ASK YOU... MA!
...YOU MAY...
ASK AWAY...
...BUT FIRST, WE NEED TO TAME NINE TAILS!
WHEEEEE
UGH!
ZW ZW ZW
ZW
ZW ZW ZW
WHOOSH

?!
SWRRRRRRL
THUNK
KUSHINA ...!
G-G-G-G-G-G-G-G
?!
THIS CHAKRA...

MINATO SPELLED MY CHAKRA INTO THE SEALING JUTSU SO I'D APPEAR...
...WHEN YOU TRIED TO GAIN CONTROL OVER NINE TAILS' POWER.
SO THAT I COULD LEND YOU A HAND...
?
HEH HEH HEH...
ARE YOU LISTENING?
YOU'RE BEAUTIFUL, MA!
WELL, THANK YOU!
TEE HEE...
YOU HAVE YOUR FATHER'S HAIR, BUT I'M SORRY YOU HAVE MY FACE, NARUTO.
WHY?
I GOT MY GOOD LOOKS FROM YOU, RIGHT?
I EVEN WISH I HAD GOTTEN YOUR STRAIGHT RED HAIR. IT'S AWESOME!

READ THIS WAY

HOW DID YOU MEET PA?
...!
I-IT'S... A BIT EMBARRASSING, YA KNOW...?!
HEY, YOU SAID YA KNOW LIKE I DO!
YOU'RE TALKING FAST AGAIN!
YEP, I'M GETTING MY THOUGHTS WOUND UP, YA KNOW!
YOU SAID IT AGAIN, A-HA HA HA!
...

READ THIS WAY

IT'S PRETTY SNOTTY TO DECLARE YOU'RE GOING TO BECOME HOKAGE AFTER JUST MOVING FROM ANOTHER VILLAGE, RIGHT?
SO I STARTED GETTING TAUNTED BY BOYS... AND THEY NICKNAMED ME TOMATO!
TOMATO? WHY?
BECAUSE I WAS CHUBBY, WITH A ROUND FACE AND RED HAIR...
I GUESS IT WAS ACTUALLY PRETTY ACCURATE.
I BET PA TOTALLY PUT A STOP TO THAT.
RIGHT?!
NOPE...! GUESS AGAIN!
SHF
ANYBODY WHO CALLED ME TOMATO...WELL, I JUST TURNED THEM INTO SMASHED TOMATOES.
THAT'S HOW I GOT MY OTHER NICKNAME...
THE RED-HOT HABANERO!!
NOW I REMEMBER KIBA AND SHIKAMARU SAYING THAT MOTHERS CAN BE REAL SCARY...
ULP

READ THIS WAY
SO... WHAT DID PA WANT TO BE WHEN HE GREW UP?
MINATO? THIS IS WHAT HE SAID...
...
I WANT TO BECOME A GREAT HOKAGE! EVERYONE IN THE WHOLE VILLAGE WILL RESPECT ME!
...
A HOKAGE... RESPECTED BY EVERY-ONE... HUH.
WHEN I FIRST HEARD HIM SAY THAT...
...I MOCKED MINATO, THINKING HE SEEMED SO UNDEPENDABLE THAT THERE WAS NO WAY HE'D EVER BECOME HOKAGE.
WHAT?!
BUT PA SEEMS SO POWER-FUL!
...I KNOW.
WELL, I WAS STILL YOUNG AND DIDN'T KNOW ANYTHING BACK THEN, SO I LOOKED DOWN ON MINATO.
UNTIL A CERTAIN INCIDENT.

?
...A CERTAIN INCIDENT ...?
I USED TO REALLY HATE MY RED HAIR...
...BUT SINCE THAT INCIDENT, I LIKED IT... THANKS TO MINATO.
WHAT HAP-PENED?
I HAVE A SLIGHTLY SPECIAL CHAKRA...
...AND WAS KIDNAPPED BY THE VILLAGE OF KUMOGAKURE BECAUSE OF IT.
IN ORDER TO LEAVE BEHIND A TRAIL, WHILE I WAS BEING LED AWAY...
...I SNIPPED OFF AND DROPPED STRANDS OF MY HAIR.
CAREFULLY, SO THE ENEMY WOULDN'T NOTICE...
SNIP

READ THIS WAY

MY HAIR BECAME MY RED DESTINY.
AND SINCE THEN, I'VE LIKED MY HAIR...
...AND MOST OF ALL, I FELL IN LOVE WITH MINATO.
THERE ARE CERTAIN WORDS I ONLY BESTOW ON THE MEN WHO COMPLIMENT MY HAIR...
...WILL YOU ACCEPT THEM, NARUTO?
?
SURE...
ZING
ZING...

I LOVE YOU.
...
IF YOU PUT THE YELLOW FLASH OF KONOHA TOGETHER WITH THE RED-HOT HABANERO...
HEH HEH...
TA-
YOU GET KONOHA'S ORANGE HOKAGE!!
DAA
FSH...

Number 499: A New Seal!!

...SO HAPPY!!!
RAAAAR!!
KUSHINA...!
ZWW...
ZWWW...

ZWOOOOOSH
HO HO...
WHAT?
SWOOO...
THIS IS REAL NICE! FOR NOW, KEEPING WATCH WILL SUFFICE!
SWSH
MY CHAKRA SUPPRESSING NINE TAILS WON'T LAST TOO MUCH LONGER...
SO GO ON AND GET HIM!
YSH
YES, MA'AM!
ART OF THE SHADOW DOPPEL-GANGER!!

B-B-BOOF
...YOU BRAT!
RRRRRRR
HERE I GO!!
TAK TAK TAK TAK
UNNNNNH
CREAK CREAK
RRRIP

READ THIS WAY
HE REALLY IS STRONG!
SLOSH
SLOSH
SLOSH
SLOSH
SLOSH
TAKE THIS!!
RAAWR !!
RASENGAN SUPER BARRAGE!!

ASH
BOOF
B-
B-
B-
B-
B-
SKY
YOU HAVEN'T WON YET!!
I'VE STILL GOT SOME JUICE!
YOINK
CRUMP...
AM
SL
?!
THIS IS IT!!

READ THIS WAY

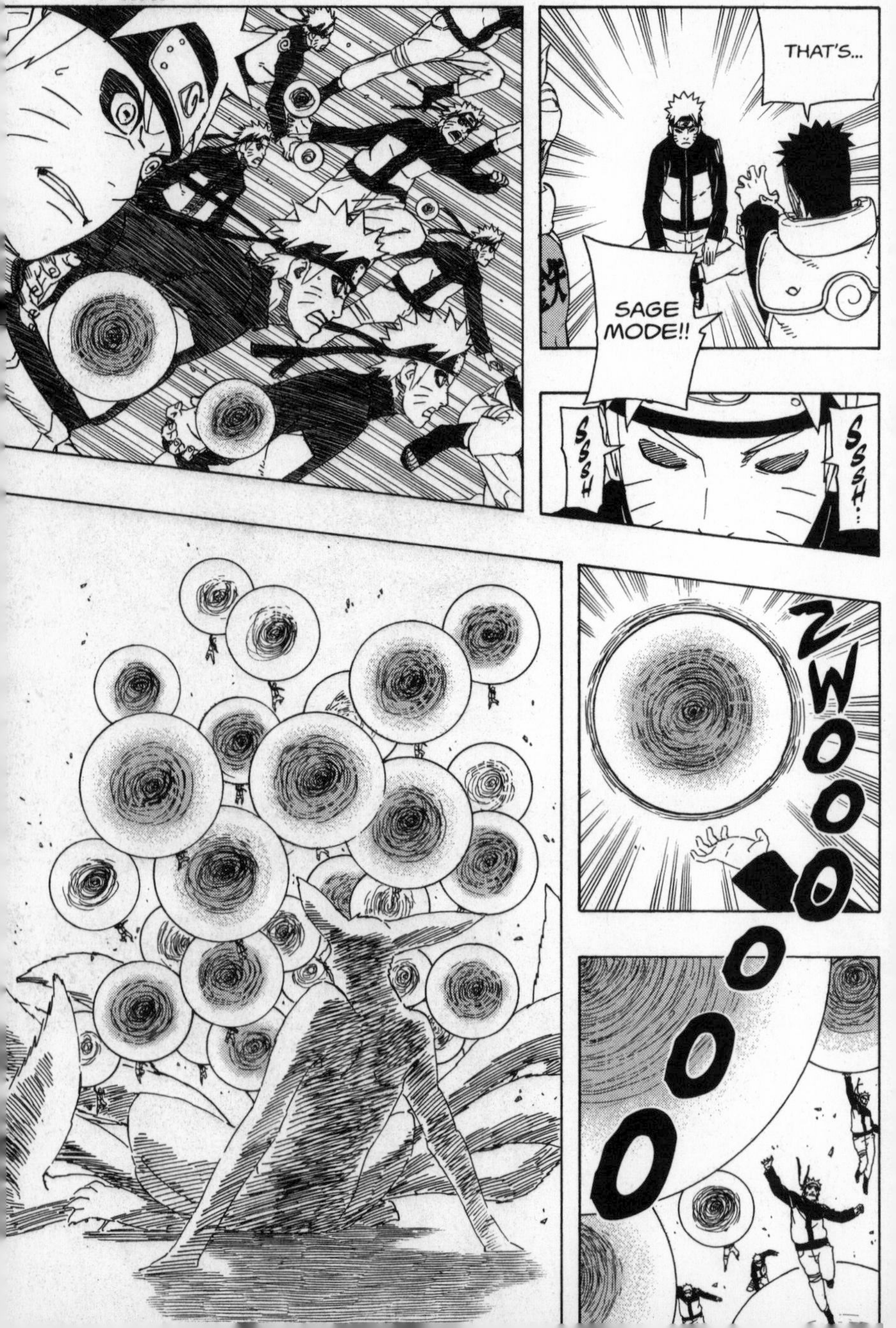

AAARGH!!
BOOF
BOOF
BOOF
BOOF
VOOSH
SWOOOOO...

SAGE ART! SUPER ÔDAMA RASENGAN BARRAGE!!
SCREECH

BOOF
TMP
SPLASH SPLASH
!
ONE MORE ROUND !!
BLAM
!
WHAT?!
WHAT KIND OF POWER IS THIS...?!

G-G-G- G-G- G
ZWOO
RAWR
RAAR!! GET OUT!!
PULL!!
RUUUUUUU...
SHWOOP
D-D-D-D-D-D

GRR...
WHUMP
B-B-B-OOF
BOOF
BOOF
BOOF
FSSSSH
FSSSSH
GRRR
SWOOOOOOOOOOOO

SWOP
BZP
BZP BZP
BZP BZP
BZP
NARUTO... YOU DARE...!

ZWIP
YOU HAVE IN-FURIATED ME! NARUTO!!
FSSSSH FSSSSH
FSSSSH FSSSSH
YOU STILL HAVE THIS MUCH POWER...?
ZWOO...
WOW... YOU REALLY ARE AMAZING...
CLAMP
WHIRL

THOOOM
DNK DNK DNK DNK
DNK
!!
THOOM
...ISN'T THIS... THE SIX PATHS'...?!
KLONG!!

...YOU WATCH OUT... NARUTO...
KLANK
...SORRY, NINE TAILS... BUT...
...I PROMISE I WON'T DO WRONG BY YOU...
SO JUST HANG IN THERE... FOR A LITTLE WHILE.
WSH...
YOU DID IT, NARUTO!
...YEAH...
SHUNK
MA, WHAT ARE YOU...
NOW I CAN FINALLY JOIN MINATO...
...!

READ THIS WAY

FSSSSH
FSSSSH.
GRRR

Number 500: The Birth of Naruto

YOU WERE NINE TAILS' JINCHÛRIKI ...
...MA?!
I WAS.
BEFORE I CAN TELL YOU THAT STORY, WHAT HAPPENED 16 YEARS AGO...
...YOU NEED TO KNOW MORE ABOUT ME.
I WAS SELECTED AS THE SECOND JINCHÛRIKI HOST OF NINE TAILS.
THEY BROUGHT ME TO KONOHA... ALL THE WAY FROM THE LAND OF EDDIES.
LAND OF EDDIES
LAND OF FIRE
GRRR
...
WHY ...?!
YOU WERE A STRANGER FROM ANOTHER NATION. WHY WERE YOU A JINCHÛRIKI ?!
(FIRE)
火
(EDDIES)
渦
YES. I WAS FROM A DIFFERENT HIDDEN VILLAGE. ANOTHER NATION.
BUT BACK THEN, THE LAND OF FIRE AND THE LAND OF EDDIES HAD A VERY CLOSE RELATIONSHIP.

THE SHINOBI OF KONOHA'S SENJU CLAN AND UZUSHIO'S UZUMAKI CLAN WERE DISTANT BLOOD RELATIVES.
FULL OF SHINOBI BRIMMING WITH VITALITY, UZUSHIO VILLAGE WAS ALSO KNOWN AS THE VILLAGE OF LONGEVITY.
THE CLANFOLK EXCELLED AT SEALING JUTSU. BUT THEY WERE ALSO A BIT SAVAGE.
THE TETRAGRAM SEAL ON YOUR BELLY WAS BASED ON A JUTSU ORIGINALLY DEVELOPED BY MY VILLAGE.
I TAUGHT IT TO MINATO, YOUR FATHER, ALONG WITH OTHER SEALING JUTSU.
NARUTO, THAT SYMBOL ON THE BACK OF YOUR JACKET...
...IS THE CREST OF UZUSHIO-GAKURE VILLAGE.
IT SYMBOLIZES TO THIS DAY THE CAMARADERIE BETWEEN KONOHA AND UZUSHIO...

...EVEN THOUGH UZUSHIO NO LONGER EXISTS AS A NATION NOW.
DURING THE ERA OF WAR AND UNREST, OUR SEALING JUTSU ABILITIES WERE GREATLY FEARED. WE WERE TARGETED AND ERADICATED.
SURVIVORS FLED AND HID THEMSELVES THROUGHOUT THE LANDS.
BUT...
...WHY **YOU**, MA...?!
IN FACT, THE FIRST NINE TAILS JINCHÛRIKI WAS ALSO AN UZUSHIO *KUNOICHI*.
WHICH MADE IT TRADITION.
I WAS BORN WITH A PARTICULARLY POWERFUL CHAKRA. STRONG EVEN FOR ONE FROM MY VILLAGE. STRONG ENOUGH TO SUPPRESS NINE TAILS.
HER NAME WAS UZUMAKI MITO, AND SHE WAS THE WIFE OF THE FIRST HOKAGE.
SO I DECIDED THAT I'D BE THE WIFE OF THE FOURTH HOKAGE.
...
DO YOU KNOW ABOUT THE BATTLE BETWEEN FIRST HOKAGE LORD SENJU HASHIRAMA AND UCHIHA MADARA?
YEAH.

IT WAS DURING THAT BATTLE THAT IN ORDER TO LEND STRENGTH TO LORD HASHIRAMA, WHO HAD OBTAINED NINE TAILS...
...LADY MITO SEALED NINE TAILS INSIDE HERSELF USING SEALING JUTSU AND BECAME NINE TAILS' JINCHÛRIKI.
EVER SINCE, KONOHA HAS POSSESSED NINE TAILS...
WHEN LADY MITO APPROACHED THE END OF HER LIFE...
...I WAS BROUGHT IN TO BECOME NINE TAILS' NEXT VESSEL.
THEY WEREN'T EVEN TREAT-ING YOU LIKE A PERSON?!
I WAS BROUGHT TO KONOHA WITHOUT BEING TOLD THE TRUTH.
OF COURSE, I WAS COMPLETELY SHOCKED WHEN I FOUND OUT.
EVERY-THING WAS TOP SECRET.
THE ONLY ONES WHO KNEW WERE LORD THIRD AND A FEW OF THE ELDERS. NOT EVEN THE THREE GREAT SHINOBI KNEW.
I WAS SO LONELY. THE RESPONSIBILITY ALMOST RUINED ME.
BUT THEN LADY MITO TOLD ME...
?
...THAT THOUGH WE BOTH CAME TO KONOHA TO BECOME JINCHÛRIKI...

...THE KEY WAS TO FILL OURSELVES WITH LOVE, FIRST.
THEN, EVEN IF WE HAD TO LIVE AS NINE TAILS' JINCHÛRIKI, WE COULD STILL BE HAPPY.
... THEN, MA...?
YOU WERE A JINCHÛRIKI... BUT YOU WERE HAPPY...?!
YUP!
...
SNIFF...
HEH HEH ...
SQUICH

READ THIS WAY

WHAT HAPPENED ?!
THAT MASKED MAN... I DON'T KNOW HOW, BUT HE *KNEW*...
...!
KNEW WHAT?
ABOUT THE ONE AND ONLY TIME THAT A JINCHÛRIKI BIJU SEAL WEAKENS.
HE TIMED HIS ATTACK PERFECTLY. AND HE STOLE NINE TAILS FROM ME.
THE ONE TIME THE SEAL WEAKENS?!
WHEN'S THAT?!
CHILD-BIRTH.

DURING THE APPROXIMATELY TEN MONTHS BETWEEN WHEN A FEMALE JINCHÛRIKI GETS PREGNANT AND GIVES BIRTH...
THE BIJU SEAL WEAKENS PROPORTIONALLY AS THE ENERGY...
...THAT IS NORMALLY USED FOR THE SEAL IS DIVERTED TO THE GROWING BABY.
THEN...
OCTOBER 10, 16 YEARS AGO.
I'LL BE THERE WHEN SHE GIVES BIRTH. I MUST MONITOR THE SEAL, ANYWAY.
I'LL GO ON AHEAD AND GET THINGS READY.
IT WAS THAT WAY WITH LADY MITO TOO...
WHEN SHE GAVE BIRTH, THE SEAL ALMOST CAME COMPLETELY UNDONE.

I APOLOGIZE, BUT CONSIDERING THE WORST-CASE SCENARIO, WE'VE DECIDED TO HAVE YOU GIVE BIRTH INSIDE A BARRIER AT A SLIGHT DISTANCE FROM THE VILLAGE.
MINATO, MY WIFE BIWAKO, AND TAJI OF THE BLACK OPS WILL ACCOMPANY YOU...
...AND ALL THIS WILL BE TOP SECRET.
YOU'LL HAVE GUARDS AS WELL. THEY'LL ALL BE BLACK OPS DIRECTLY ASSIGNED TO ME...
I SHALL GUIDE YOU TO THE LOCATION. WE'LL BE HEADING OUT SHORTLY!
YES... THANK YOU VERY MUCH.
古書
HUH? YOU HAD A GIRL?
NO. BOY.
WHAT DID YOU NAME HIM, MIKOTO?

SASUKE.
AH, THE SAME AS THE THIRD'S FATHER.
YES. SO HE GROWS UP TO BE A STRONG, SPLENDID SHINOBI.
YOU'RE DUE PRETTY SOON, AREN'T YOU, KUSHINA? YOU OUGHT TO START PICKING NAMES.
WE'VE ALREADY DECIDED ON NARUTO.
HE'LL BE YEAR-MATES WITH SASUKE, SO I HOPE THEY GET ALONG.
DOES IT REALLY HURT LIKE THEY SAY?
FSH
WOW... THERE'S ACTUALLY SOMETHING THAT SCARES YOU?!
WHAT A SHOCK!
COME, LET'S GO, KUSHINA!
YES, MA'AM!
SHF...
LATER...!
THE DETAILS OF YOUR BIRTHING ARE TOP SECRET, REMEMBER?
UNTIL THE DAY WE MOVE YOU, YOU ARE TO MINIMIZE ALL CONTACT WITH EVEN YOUR FRIENDS.
YES, MA'AM... SORRY.
FURTHER-MORE... ALTHOUGH WE WILL BE OUTSIDE THE VILLAGE, WE'LL STILL BE MAINTAINING COVERT STATUS!
SO EVEN WHEN YOUR LABOR PAINS START, YOU ARE NOT TO RAISE YOUR VOICE, UNDER-STAND?!
OH... YES, MA'AM...!

封
AAAARGH ...!!! IT HURTS, YA KNOW ...!!!
UGH...!!
UM, I'VE NEVER SEEN KUSHINA CRY OUT IN PAIN.
IS THIS REALLY OKAY?
SHE'S FINE! YOU JUST STAY FOCUSED ON NINE TAILS' SEAL!
BUT SHE'S...
YOU'RE THE FOURTH HOKAGE!! GET A GRIP!!
結
MOST MEN WOULD HAVE DROPPED DEAD FROM SUCH PAIN LONG AGO, BUT WOMEN ARE MUCH STRONGER!!
!
ZWW

RAAR
!!
UNNNH ...!!
HE'S STRONG! NINE TAILS IS WRITHING TO GET OUT!!
HANG IN THERE, KUSHINA!
COME ON, NARUTO!!
SSH
封

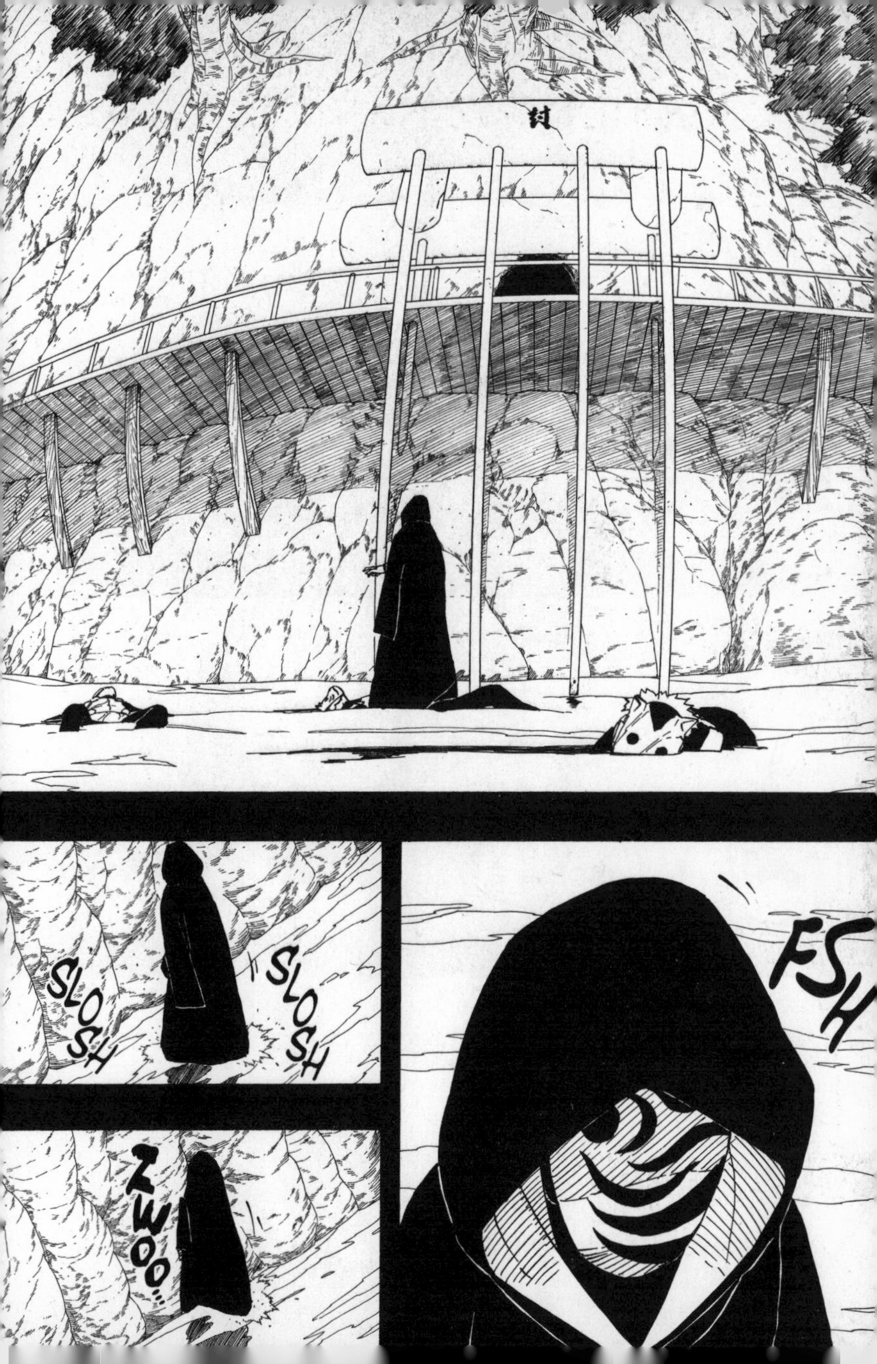

封
SLOSH SLOSH
SLOSH SLOSH
FSH
TWOO...

UGGH...!
THE HEAD'S OUT!! JUST A WEE BIT MORE, KUSHINA!
HANG IN THERE, KUSHINA!!
RAAAR
NARUTO! HURRY UP AND COME OUT!
YOU STAY IN, NINE TAILS!!
UNNH...!!
WAAH!!
WAAH!!
...
HE'S HERE...
HOT WATER!
YES, MA'AM!
HUF!
HUF!
HUF!

WAAAH WAAAH!!
IT'S A HEALTHY BABY BOY!!
HA HA...!
I'M A FATHER NOW...!!
NARUTO ...
HUF
WE FINALLY MEET...
WAAH WAAH

ALL RIGHT, KUSHINA!
IT'S ROUGH HAVING JUST GIVEN BIRTH... BUT WE NEED TO COMPLETELY SUPPRESS NINE TAILS AGAIN!
HUF
HUF
SHUP
YEAH...
AARGH!!
AIEE!
!!
LADY BIWAKO! TAJI!
FOURTH HOKAGE MINATO...
STEP AWAY FROM THE JINCHÛRIKI...
FSH
...OR ELSE THIS CHILD WILL DIE AFTER ITS FIRST MINUTE.

NARUTO

Number 501: Nine Tails Attacks!!

WAAAAH
WAAAAH
HOW DID HE GET PAST THE BARRIER ...?!
WHO IS HE...?!
RRRNK...
UGH!
UNH...
WRRRR
KUSHINA!
...NINE TAILS' SEAL ISN'T...!

HURRY UP AND STEP AWAY FROM THE JINCHÛRIKI ...
DON'T YOU CARE WHAT HAPPENS TO YOUR BRAT?
SHP
BLIP...
BLOOP...
WAIT... STAY CALM!
UGH... UNH!
SPEAK FOR YOURSELF. I'M SUPREMELY CALM, MINATO.
WOOSH
NARUTO!!

TMP
LEAVE IT TO THE YELLOW FLASH...
...BUT WHAT ABOUT NEXT?
FSSS
!!
VW-VWOOSH
WUP
YOINK

MINATO!
NARUTO !!
BO M
SCREECH
...PHEW...
WAAH! WAAH!
NARUTO'S NOT HURT...
OW...
SIGH ...

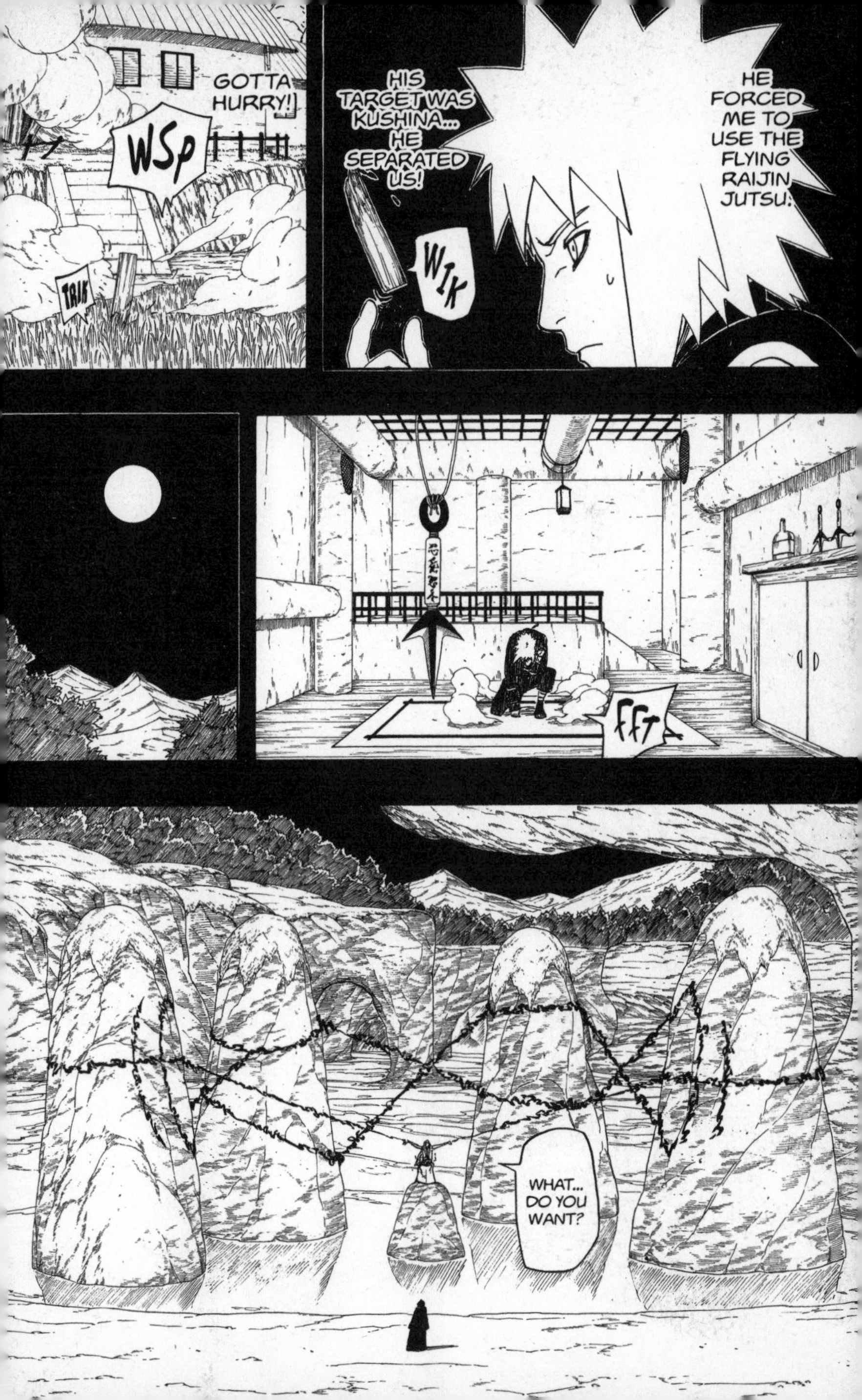
HE FORCED ME TO USE THE FLYING RAIJIN JUTSU.
HIS TARGET WAS KUSHINA... HE SEPARATED US!
WIK
GOTTA HURRY!!
WSP
TRIK
FFT
WHAT... DO YOU WANT?

I'M GOING TO EXTRACT NINE TAILS FROM YOU AND CRUSH KONOHA.
HUF
HUF
WHAT...?!
MINATO'S ART OF TELEPORTATION ALLOWS HIM TO TRANSPORT BETWEEN LOCATIONS MARKED WITH JUTSU SYMBOLS.
THE MARKINGS ARE INCORPORATED INTO THIS SEALING SPELL.
MINATO CAN PROTECT YOU AT ALL TIMES.
BUT HE IS FAR AWAY RIGHT NOW.
GRRRR
NINE TAILS' SEAL HAS WEAKENED DUE TO CHILDBIRTH.
DO YOU KNOW HOW LONG I HAVE WAITED FOR THIS?
ZOT
!!
YOU'LL BE SAFE HERE.
PLEASE BE PATIENT, NARUTO.
I HAVE TO RESCUE YOUR MOTHER...
FSH...

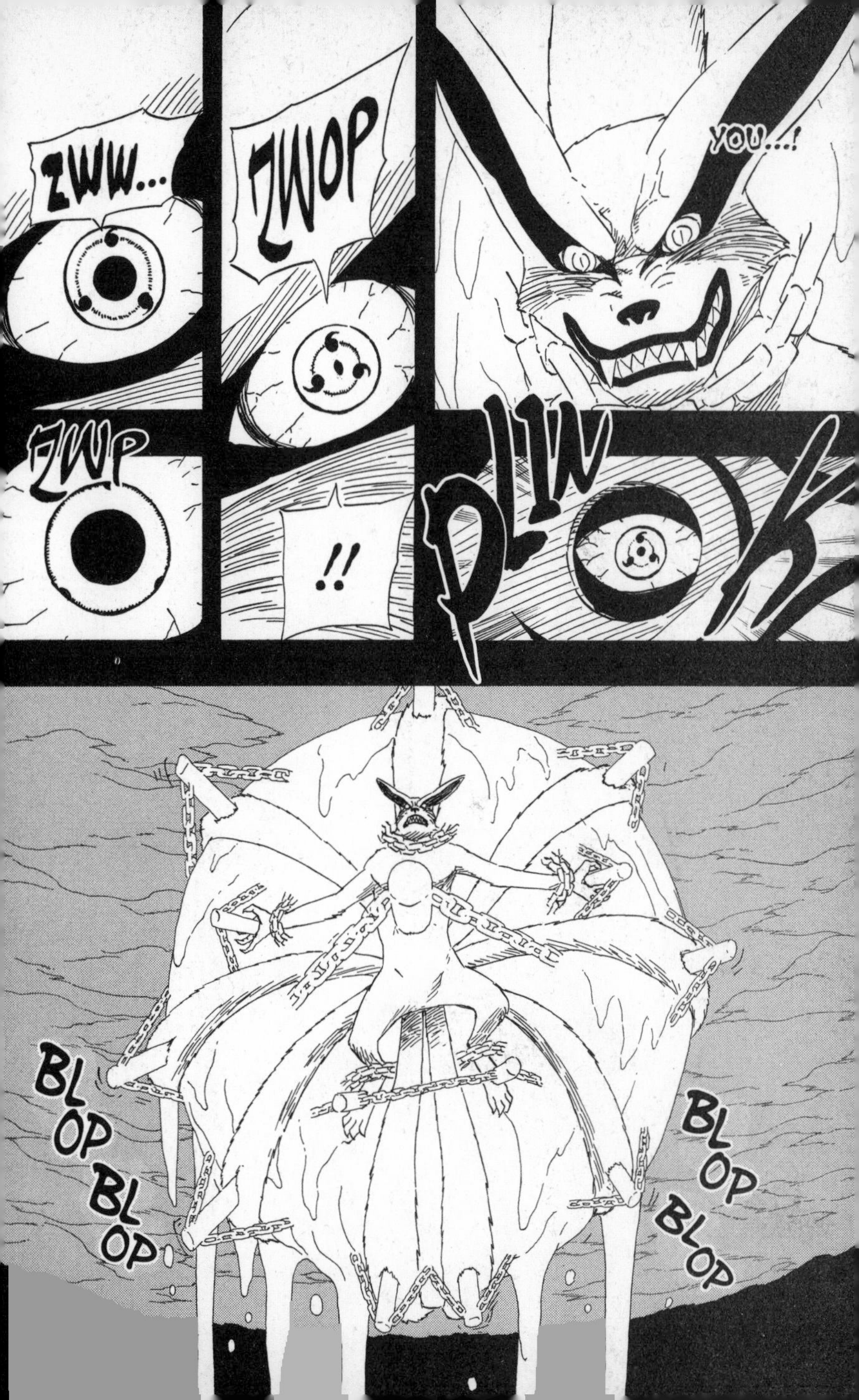
YOU...!
ZWOP
ZWW...
!!
ZWP
PLINK
BLOP BLOP
BLOP BLOP

BLOOOO...
RAAAR!!!
ZWWW
BLP
GLUP GLUP
ZWOOO
ZWUP
NOW... COME ON OUT, NINE TAILS!

DOM

RAAAAAR!!!

BZP
BZP
SHUP
GOOD... TO KONOHA-GAKURE!
UGH...
WAIT...
HUF
HUF
FSH
RAAAAR!
YOU UZUMAKI SHINOBI ARE JUST AMAZING...
...YOU DON'T DIE RIGHT AWAY WHEN THE BIJU IS EXTRACTED?

YOU WERE HIS JINCHÛRIKI ...
...I'LL LET YOU DIE BY HIS HAND.
!!
BAM

TMP
YOU REALLY ARE A FLASH...
...BUT YOU'RE TOO LATE.
HUF
...MINATO...
...NARUTO... IS NARUTO... ALL RIGHT?
HUF
YEAH... HE'S FINE... HE'S IN A SAFE PLACE RIGHT NOW...
...OH, GOOD...
GRRR
MINATO... STOP THAT MAN AND NINE TAILS...
...THEY'RE PLANNING... TO HIT KONOHA ...
HUF
HUF

...
WSP
...HE FLEW AWAY...
THAT'S FINE... NOW LET'S GET TO KONOHA.
SWSH
!
WHY...?
FSH...
SHH... JUST BE WITH NARUTO...
...
HUF
HUF
SNOO
SNOO

NARUTO...
...
FSH
GRK
YOWK
MINATO... THANK YOU...
...GOOD LUCK...

...I'LL BE RIGHT BACK...
FW
四代目火影
AP
!
I FEEL SOME-THING OMINOUS... WHAT IS IT?

NARUTO

Number 502: The Fourth Lord's Death Match!!

UNNH...
STRANGE FEELING...
WAAA AAH!
NOW, NOW...
OF COURSE, FATHER AND MOTHER HAVE TO BE OUT...
DON'T CRY, SASUKE...
NO MATTER WHAT HAPPENS, YOUR BIG BRO WILL PROTECT YOU...
西酒場
HMM...? WHY DON'T WE JUST DO ROCK, PAPER, SCISSORS AGAIN FOR TODAY?
NO WAY! ISN'T THERE SOMETHING MORE BLOOD-BOILING THAT WE COULD TRY?!
YOU CALL YOURSELF MY RIVAL?!

...
A SUDDEN CHILL IN THE AIR...
FORGET ALL THAT, GUY. DON'T YOU FEEL SOMETHING WEIRD?
ONLY THING CHILLY IS YOUR ATTITUDE!
WE'RE ONLY YOUNG ONCE, YOU KNOW!
ZAP
IT CAN'T BE...
ART OF SUMMON-ING...!

OO
M
RAAAAR!!
THD-
THD-
THD-
THD-

TH
AARGH !!
WHAT ?!
...!
TH- THAT'S...
GO, NINE TAILS!
LORD THIRD HOKAGE !!
IT'S NINE TAILS! NINE TAILS IS INSIDE THE VILLAGE!
TMP

I KNOW! I'LL RESTRAIN HIM! YOU ALL GO ON AND PROTECT THE CIVILIANS!
YES, SIR!
WAS KUSHINA'S SEAL RELEASED?
WE FAILED EVEN WITH ALL THE SAFE-GUARDS?!
SQK
TMP
PHOO OM...
TMP
!!

NOTICED ME?
I WON'T LET YOU DESTROY THIS SPOT!!
FWP
FWP

THO
OM
ZWOOO...
KABO
OM
WITH THIS MUCH POWER, I'VE GOT TO CAREFULLY CHOOSE WHERE I REDIRECT HIS ATTACKS...
RUMBLE
THE JUTSU THAT DEFLECTED NINE TAILS' ATTACK... THAT WAS A TELEPORTATION BARRIER!
IT'S GOT TO BE MINATO!

ALL RIGHT! LET'S GO TOO!!
GRR
YES, SIR!!
I'VE GOT TO ALERT LORD THIRD RIGHT AWAY ABOUT WHAT'S GOING ON...
!
SWSH
!!

I'M YOUR OPPONENT.
CH AK
AND... YOU'RE DONE FOR.
ZWOOOOOOOOOOOOOOOOOO
WSP
...!!
HE GOT AWAY...
...SO FAST...
NEXT TIME, I'LL TAKE HIM A LOT QUICKER... AS SOON AS WE TOUCH...

THUD
UGH...!
MY ATTACK PASSED RIGHT THROUGH HIM...
A MOMENT LATER, HE MADE HIMSELF SOLID AND TRIED TO PULL ME INSIDE OF HIM... WHAT WAS THAT JUTSU?
ZWWW...
?!
YOU SHALL NOT ESCAPE.
ZWOP
ZWOP
FSH
HE USES TELEPORTATION NINJUTSU TOO?!
SO THAT'S HOW HE WAS ABLE TO GRAB KUSHINA AND MOVE SO QUICKLY!
HE MANAGED TO DEFEAT THE BLACK OPS DIRECTLY ASSIGNED TO LORD THIRD, GET PAST THE HIGHEST-LEVEL CLASSIFIED BARRIER...
...KNEW THAT NINE TAILS' SEAL WOULD WEAKEN DURING CHILD-BIRTH...
...PLUS WAS ABLE TO UNRAVEL NINE TAILS' SEAL, TAME HIM...
...AND SLIP IN AND OUT OF KONOHA'S BARRIERS WITHOUT TRIGGERING ANY ALARMS. AS FAR AS I KNOW, THERE IS ONLY ONE SHINOBI WHO CAN DO ALL THAT...

ARE YOU UCHIHA MADARA?
FSH
BUT NO... IT'S NOT POSSIBLE...
HE'S DEAD.
HMM... I WONDER ABOUT THAT...
IN THE END, IT DOESN'T MATTER WHO YOU ARE...
BUT WHY ATTACK KONOHA?
IT SEEMS... WHIMSICAL... BUT ALSO SOMEWHAT PLANNED...
FOR THE SAKE OF WAR... BUT ALSO FOR THE SAKE OF PEACE.
RATTLE...
...
EITHER WAY... HE'S NOT ORDINARY! HE CAN CONTROL NINE TAILS. HIS TELEPORTATION NINJUTSU SURPASSES BOTH THE SECOND LORD'S AND MINE... AND HE'S GOT SOME DANGEROUS IDEOLOGY...
IF I DON'T SETTLE THIS, WE'LL HAVE BIGGER PROBLEMS THAN NINE TAILS.
FSH

IF I TRANSPORT MYSELF TO THE VILLAGE... HE'LL COME TO THE BATTLEFIELD WITH ME... IT'LL BE CHAOS...
IF HE'S ANYTHING LIKE MADARA, HE SHOULDN'T BE ABLE TO MAINTAIN NINE TAILS IN REAL SPACE FOR THAT LONG...
I HAVE TO ENTRUST THE VILLAGE TO THE THIRD LORD... AND JUST TAKE THIS GUY DOWN RIGHT HERE, RIGHT NOW!!
THERE IS NO HOPE FOR YOU!
!!
RATTLE
CLINK

?!!
SWSH
TMP
KLATTER...
MY PHYSICAL ATTACKS DON'T AFFECT HIS BODY... BUT HE MAKES HIMSELF SOLID WHEN HE ATTACKS ME...
I HAVE TO AIM FOR A MUTUAL STRIKE, PRECISELY TIMED!
HE KNOWS HE'S VULNERABLE WHEN HE ATTACKS.
IT TAKES A LONG TIME TO SUMMON NINE TAILS. HE WON'T WANT A LENGTHY BATTLE.
TA
K
THIS IS ALL GOING TO BE OVER FOR ONE OF US IN AN INSTANT!
TA
K

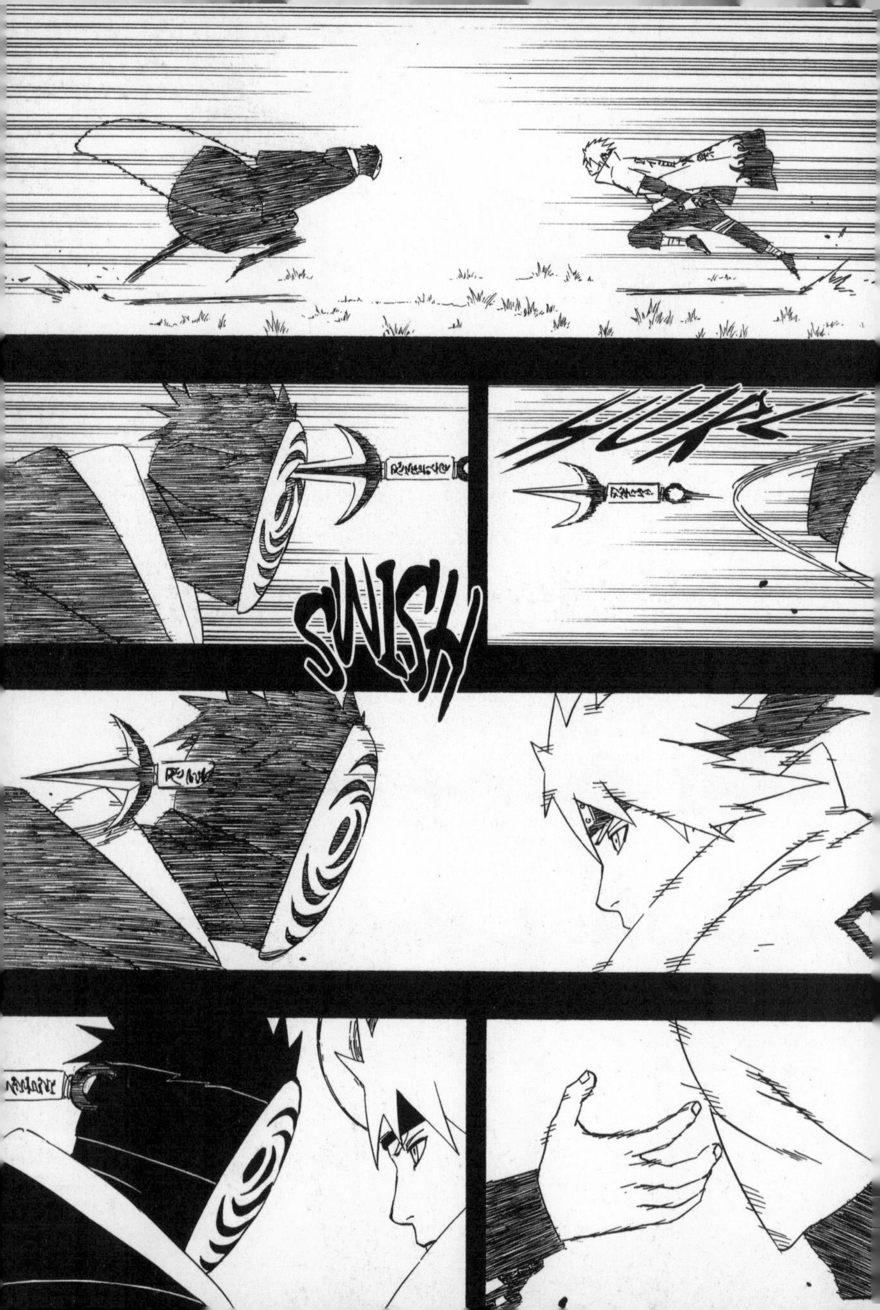
HURL
SWISH

四代目火影
I WIN...
WSP

GAK!!
RASEN-GAN!!
SLAM
HE TRANSPORTED HIMSELF TO THE POSITION OF HIS KUNAI!!
CHAK
FLYING RAIJIN, LEVEL 2.

Number
503:
Minato's
Reaper
Death
Seal!!

NARUTO

KA-BOOM
UGH!
SH
OOO
TMP
PLIIP...
SKROOSH

?!!
KL
ANG
四代目火影
UGH!
FLYING RAIJIN JUTSU!!
HE MUST HAVE PLANTED SYMBOLS ON ME!!

WHAMM
!!
A CONTRACT SEAL!!
TRYING TO SEPARATE NINE TAILS FROM ME?!
NINE TAILS IS NO LONGER YOURS!
RAAAR!!
SWOOOOO
FSH

IRUKA... ARE YOU ALL RIGHT...?
BABUMP BABUMP
MA...
PA! MA'S...!!
LEAVE YOUR MA TO ME!
YOU GO HIDE, NOW!!
NO!! I DON'T WANNA LEAVE YOU AND MA BEHIND!!
I'LL DEFEND MA!
DON'T PUSH ME, BOY!!
IT'S THE PARENTS' DUTY TO PROTECT THEIR CHILDREN!!
...!

KABOOM...
THOOM...
MINATO, WHERE ARE YOU?!
WE'VE DRIVEN HIM OUT OF THE VILLAGE!
NOW KEEP AT HIM, ONE AFTER ANOTHER!
TAK TAK TAK TAK TAK

YOU'RE WORTHY OF YOUR TITLE, FOURTH HOKAGE, INFLICTING INJURY UPON ME AND SEPARATING NINE TAILS FROM ME...
BUT HE WILL BE MINE FOR GOOD ONE DAY...
I SHALL RULE THIS WORLD...
THERE ARE PLENTY OF WAYS TO GO ABOUT IT.
SWOOO...
GIVEN HIS TONE...
...HE'S NOT JOKING AROUND.
KEEP HIM OCCUPIED UNTIL LORD FOURTH GETS HERE!
LET ME GO...!!
PA AND MA ARE STILL FIGHTING!!

LISTEN UP. YOU YOUNGER SHINOBI STAY AWAY FROM NINE TAILS...
THIS IS DOMESTIC TROUBLE, NOT A WAR AGAINST OTHER VILLAGES.
THERE IS NO NEED FOR YOU ALL TO RISK YOUR LIVES.
結
WHAT DO YOU MEAN?!
NO MORE PONTIFI-CATING!!
CALM... KURENAI!
YOU'RE ALSO SHINOBI. YOU'RE NOT GOING TO LIVE FOREVER...
BUT, DAUGHTER... YOU'RE A WOMAN TOO.
BEQUEATH THE WILL OF FIRE UPON MY FUTURE GRAND-CHILDREN!
MAKE THAT YOUR OATH TO YOUR FATHER... FOR I DO BELIEVE IN YOU.
RAAR!!
ZING

TMP
!!
OH NO...!!
UGH... HE'S GOING TO DO THAT AGAIN?!
LORD THIRD !!
WUMF
ART OF SUMMONING !!
SLAM
IT'S THE FOURTH LORD!!

...
I SHALL RULE THIS WORLD...
KUSHINA... FORGIVE ME...
HOLD NINE TAILS DOWN!
THAT'S GONNA BE TOUGH, EVEN FOR ME!
I'M GOING TO NEED A LOT OF CHAKRA TO TRANSPORT SUCH A LARGE OBJECT AWAY!
UGH!
PHOOM

...MINATO...
YOU TELE-PORTED NINE TAILS WITH YOU?!
KA
BOOM
OVER THERE!
RRRUMMBLE

HUF
I'VE GOT TO ERECT A BARRIER RIGHT AWAY...!
BUT NOT MUCH CHAKRA LEFT...
HUF
...I CAN STILL... DO IT... MINATO...
WSP
SHRR
GRRR ...
RRRRRRRRRRL

WAAAH WAAAH
KUSHINA ...!
HACK
HACK
WHOOPS... WOKE HIM UP...
HUF
HUF
SORRY... NARUTO...
KUSHINA ...
I'LL TAKE... NINE TAILS WITH ME... TO MY DEATH...
...SO THAT... THE INTERVAL UNTIL HE... EMERGES AGAIN... IS DELAYED.
IT'S ALL I CAN MANAGE RIGHT NOW, WITH MY REMAINING CHAKRA, TO HELP YOU TWO.
THANK YOU... FOR EVERY-THING UP 'TIL NOW.
!!
WAM...

...
KUSHINA... YOU'RE THE ONE...
WAAH!
WAAH!
四代目火影
...WHO MADE ME THE FOURTH HOKAGE!
AND MADE ME THIS CHILD'S FATHER!!
WHO MADE ME YOUR MAN!!
AND YET I'M USE- LESS!
MINATO... DON'T LOOK SO SAD.
I...I'M HAPPY...
I'M... YOU LOVE ME... PLUS...
WAAAH
WAAAH
...TODAY... IS THE CHILD'S BIRTHDAY... SO...

MOST OF ALL... IF...I... WERE TO IMAGINE...
...ME ALIVE, AND OUR FUTURE... TOGETHER, AS A FAMILY OF THREE... THEN...
WAAAH!
四代目火影
WAAH!
...I CAN'T SEE US... BEING ANYTHING BUT HAPPY...
DRIP...
HUF
IF I WERE ALLOWED... JUST ONE... REGRET...
WAAAH
HUF
I WISH I COULD HAVE SEEN NARUTO... GROWN UP...
...
KUSHINA... THERE'S NO NEED FOR YOU TO DIE TO KILL NINE TAILS.
PRESERVE WHAT LITTLE OF YOUR CHAKRA REMAINS FOR YOUR **REUNION** WITH NARUTO...!
HUH...?

READ THIS WAY
I'M GOING TO SEAL THE REST OF YOUR CHAKRA INSIDE NARUTO.
IT'LL BE PART OF AN EIGHT-SIGNED SEAL.
AND THEN I'LL TAKE NINE TAILS WITH ME...
...WITH THE SEALING JUTSU THAT I CAN DO, NOT BEING A JINCHÛRIKI...
...THE SHIKIFÛJIN REAPER DEATH SEAL!
...!
BUT... THAT JUTSU RESULTS IN THE CASTER'S DEATH...
FURTHERMORE... I'M ONLY GOING TO SEAL AWAY HALF OF NINE TAILS...
PARTLY BECAUSE IT'S PHYSICALLY IMPOSSIBLE TO SEAL AWAY SUCH A LARGE VOLUME OF POWER...
...BUT ALSO BECAUSE IT'S NOT STRATEGICALLY WISE...
IF YOU TAKE NINE TAILS WITH YOU, THERE WILL BE NO JINCHÛRIKI UNTIL HE REEMERGES, AND THE BIJU BALANCE WILL BE UPSET, WHICH ISN'T GOOD.
WITH THE REAPER DEATH SEAL, WE CAN AT LEAST SEAL AWAY HALF OF NINE TAILS FOREVER.
AND THE OTHER HALF...
PERHAPS... YOU'RE THE CHILD OF PROPHECY...
HUH? THE WHAT?
IN THE FUTURE... TERRIBLE THINGS ARE LIKELY TO BEFALL THE SHINOBI WORLD.
AND THE SAVIOR THAT SHALL EMERGE IS THIS CHILD OF PROPHECY...

...I'M GOING TO SEAL INSIDE NARUTO!
USING THE EIGHT-SIGNED SEAL!
?!
I KNOW WHAT YOU'RE GOING TO SAY...
...BUT REMEMBER WHAT MASTER JIRAIYA SAID ABOUT WORLD UPHEAVAL...
...AND THE CALAMITIES THAT WILL ACCOMPANY THAT!
THERE ARE TWO THINGS... THAT I'VE BECOME CONVINCED OF TODAY.
THAT MASKED MAN WHO ATTACKED YOU... HE WILL BRING CATASTROPHE TO THIS WORLD!
AND THIS CHILD WILL BE THE ONE TO STOP HIM!
HE WILL OPEN UP THE FUTURE AS A JINCHÛRIKI.
I DON'T KNOW HOW, BUT I'M SURE OF IT.
!!

...BUT... MINATO...
FSH
未
SHEEP
亥
BOAR
巳
SNAKE
子
RAT
戌
DOG
卯
RABBIT
巳
SNAKE
午
HORSE
酉
ROOSTER
REAPER DEATH SEAL!!
LET'S BELIEVE IN THIS CHILD!
HE IS OUR SON, AFTER ALL!!
FW
P

NARUTO

HUF
...
HUF
AFTER THIS REAPER DEATH SEAL, I'M GOING TO SEAL YOUR CHAKRA INSIDE NARUTO...
YOU WON'T HAVE A WHOLE LOT OF TIME TO SPEND WITH GROWN-UP NARUTO...
...BUT I WANT YOU TO HELP HIM WHEN HE TRIES TO CONTROL NINE TAILS' POWER AS A JINCHÛRIKI.
HE'S OUR SON...
...WHICH IS EXACTLY WHY... I DON'T WANT HIM TO BEAR SUCH... A HEAVY BURDEN...!
...

BUT WHY... THE REAPER DEATH SEAL...?!
THERE'S NO NEED... FOR YOU TO DIE...
...JUST SO I CAN MEET GROWN-UP NARUTO... ESPECIALLY FOR SO SHORT A TIME...!!
...I'D RATHER YOU STAYED WITH NARUTO... AND WATCHED OVER HIS DEVELOPMENT... SEE!!
SO WHY...?!
WHY DOES NARUTO HAVE TO BE SACRIFICED...
...FOR THE BIJU BALANCE... FOR COUNTRY... FOR VILLAGE...?!!
AND WHY DO YOU HAVE TO SACRIFICE YOURSELF FOR MY SAKE?!!
HUF
HUF
TO FORSAKE ONE'S COUNTRY... AND ONE'S VILLAGE...
...IS THE SAME AS FORSAKING ONE'S CHILD.
YOU WHOSE BIRTH NATION IS NO MORE OUGHT TO KNOW THAT TOO WELL, NO?
HOW HARSH LIFE IS FOR THOSE WITHOUT A LAND TO CALL HOME...
BESIDES WHICH, OUR FAMILY...

...IS SHINOBI!!
...
FINALLY...
...EVEN IF I WERE TO LIVE, I'D LOSE OUT TO YOU...
四代目火影
...?
EVEN THOUGH YOU WON'T HAVE MUCH TIME WITH HIM...
...THERE'S SOMETHING ONLY YOU CAN TELL NARUTO, SOMETHING THAT I CAN'T...
THAT'S A MOTHER'S ROLE.
SO I'M NOT DOING THIS JUST FOR YOU...
...I'M DOING IT FOR NARUTO!

I WILL DIE FOR MY SON...
...IT IS MY DUTY AS HIS FATHER.
FSH
...
CLACK CLACK
ZWW...
THOSE SIGNS... DON'T TELL ME HE'S LAUNCH-ING...
...THE REAPER DEATH SEAL?!

THIRD LORD! WHAT'S HAPPEN-ING?!
TMP
GRRR...
IT'S NO USE... WE CAN'T MOVE IN ANY CLOSER. THIS BARRIER IS PREVENTING NINE TAILS FROM ESCAPING!
THEY'RE GOING TO TAKE CARE OF NINE TAILS BY THEMSELVES!
BZZ
SH
NK
WOOSH
YOU! FOURTH HOKAGE!!
ZWOP...

SEAL !!
RAAAAR!!
!
SHUDDER
HUF
HUF
HUF
...MY BODY'S GOING NUMB...
...I CAN'T BELIEVE HOW HEAVY HIS CHAKRA IS...
IT **IS** THE REAPER DEATH SEAL!
I DIDN'T THINK HE'D REALLY USE IT!
BUT NINE TAILS IS STILL ALIVE! HE COULDN'T SEAL ALL OF HIM AWAY?!
...ALTHOUGH HE DOES APPEAR SMALLER!

ALL RIGHT... NOW FOR THE EIGHT-SIGNED SEAL...
HUF
HUF
...TO SEAL THE REST OF NINE TAILS INSIDE NARUTO ...!
BO OF
GRRR
A RITUAL ALTAR! HE'S PLANNING TO SEAL ME UP AGAIN?! NOT INSIDE THAT BABY?!!
HUF
HUF
FSH
UGH...!
UNF...
HUF
HUF
SHRRL...
?!
SHRRL...
THERE YOU ARE!
TA K
HACK!
HACK!
COUGH
!
KUSHINA?!

THD
THD
KRAK

SHOOF...
SNOO... SNOO...
...I SAID I WAS HIS FATHER... DYING FOR HIM IS MY RIGHT.
...I'M HIS MOTHER. IT'S MY RIGHT TOO!
THERE'S A CHILD?!
THEY SAVED IT!!
!!
YOU ...!
SQUEEZE...
SKREECH
...FINE...
...THIS IS THE FIRST TIME... I LOST AN ARGUMENT AGAINST YOU...
IT PROVES... HOW SERIOUS YOU ARE...

THANKS, KUSHINA...
DRIBBLE
SKOOSH
ART OF SUMMONING!!
HOVER...
HM?!
BOOF
WHOA!! NINE TAILS!!
HEY, FOURTH! WHAT'S UP WITH YOU?!!
GAMATORA, I'M GOING TO GIVE YOU... THE SEAL SPELL KEY.
WHEN I'M DONE... GO STRAIGHT TO MASTER JIRAIYA... AND HAVE HIM TAKE YOU IN...
THAT'S IT...!
MINATO PLANS TO SAVE THE VILLAGE BY MAKING HIS OWN SON THE JINCHÛRIKI!
I AFFIRM THAT I'VE RECEIVED THE KEY!
AND NOW... I'M OFF!
FRRRRRRRR

BOOOF
...NOW WE'RE SAFE...
WHOOO
KLIK
...KUSHINA... I'M NOT GOING TO LAST MUCH LONGER...
I'M LAUNCHING... THE EIGHT-SIGNED SEAL NOW...
...SO I CAN PUT... SOME OF MY CHAKRA INSIDE NARUTO TOO...!
...WE WON'T BE SEEING HIM FOR A WHILE...
...SO LET'S... TELL HIM... WHAT WE WANT TO SAY TO HIM...
HUF
HUF
HUF
...
NARUTO...

DON'T BE A PICKY EATER... EAT A LOT... AND GROW WELL!
HUF
HUF
MAKE SURE... TO BATHE EVERY DAY... AND STAY WARM...
AND... DON'T STAY UP LATE... GET... PLENTY OF SLEEP...!!
PLUS... MAKE FRIENDS...
YOU DON'T NEED TONS... OKAY ...?!
JUST A FEW... THAT YOU CAN REALLY TRUST...!
AND... YOUR MA WAS BAD AT THIS... BUT STUDY HARD AND LEARN YOUR NINJUTSU...!
JUST... EVERYONE... IS GOOD AT SOME THINGS AND NOT SO GOOD AT OTHERS... SO EVEN IF... THINGS DON'T GO WELL... DON'T GET DEPRESSED, OKAY...?
...AT THE ACADEMY, RESPECT... YOUR TEACHERS AND THOSE SENIOR TO YOU...!
OH... AND... THIS IS IMPORTANT ...
...REGARDING THE THREE PROHIBITIONS OF THE SHINOBI... ESPECIALLY MONEY... BE CAREFUL ABOUT LOANING AND BORROWING...
MAKE SURE... TO STUDIOUSLY DEPOSIT... YOUR MISSION PAY...
AND... DON'T START DRINKING UNTIL YOU'RE 21... TOO MUCH SAKE IS BAD FOR YOUR BODY... SO... DRINK IN MODERATION...!
...AND... THE MOST PROBLEMATIC... GIRLS...
I'M A GIRL SO I DON'T REALLY KNOW MUCH ABOUT THIS... BUT AT SOME POINT YOU'LL NOTICE GIRLS. AND THAT'S NORMAL.
...JUST BE CAREFUL... DON'T FALL FOR THE FIRST GIRL THAT COMES YOUR WAY...
FIND SOME-ONE... LIKE ME...!!

...PLUS... SPEAKING OF THE THREE PROHIBI-TIONS...
BE WARY OF... MASTER JIRAIYA, YA KNOW...!
HUF
HUF
...
NARUTO... THERE'LL BE PLENTY OF HARD... AND PAINFUL... TIMES AHEAD...
TAKE CARE... OF YOUR-SELF...!
...MAKE SURE TO HAVE DREAMS...
...AND THE CONFIDENCE... TO MAKE THOSE DREAMS... COME TRUE...!!
...
SO MUCH! THERE'S SO... SO... MUCH...!
THERE REALLY IS... SO MUCH MORE I WANT... TO TELL YOU...
...I WANT TO BE WITH YOU LONGER... I LOVE YOU...
...
...I'M SORRY, MINATO... I TALKED TOO MUCH...
NO NO... IT'S ALL RIGHT...
NARUTO ...
MY WORDS TO YOU AS YOUR FATHER...

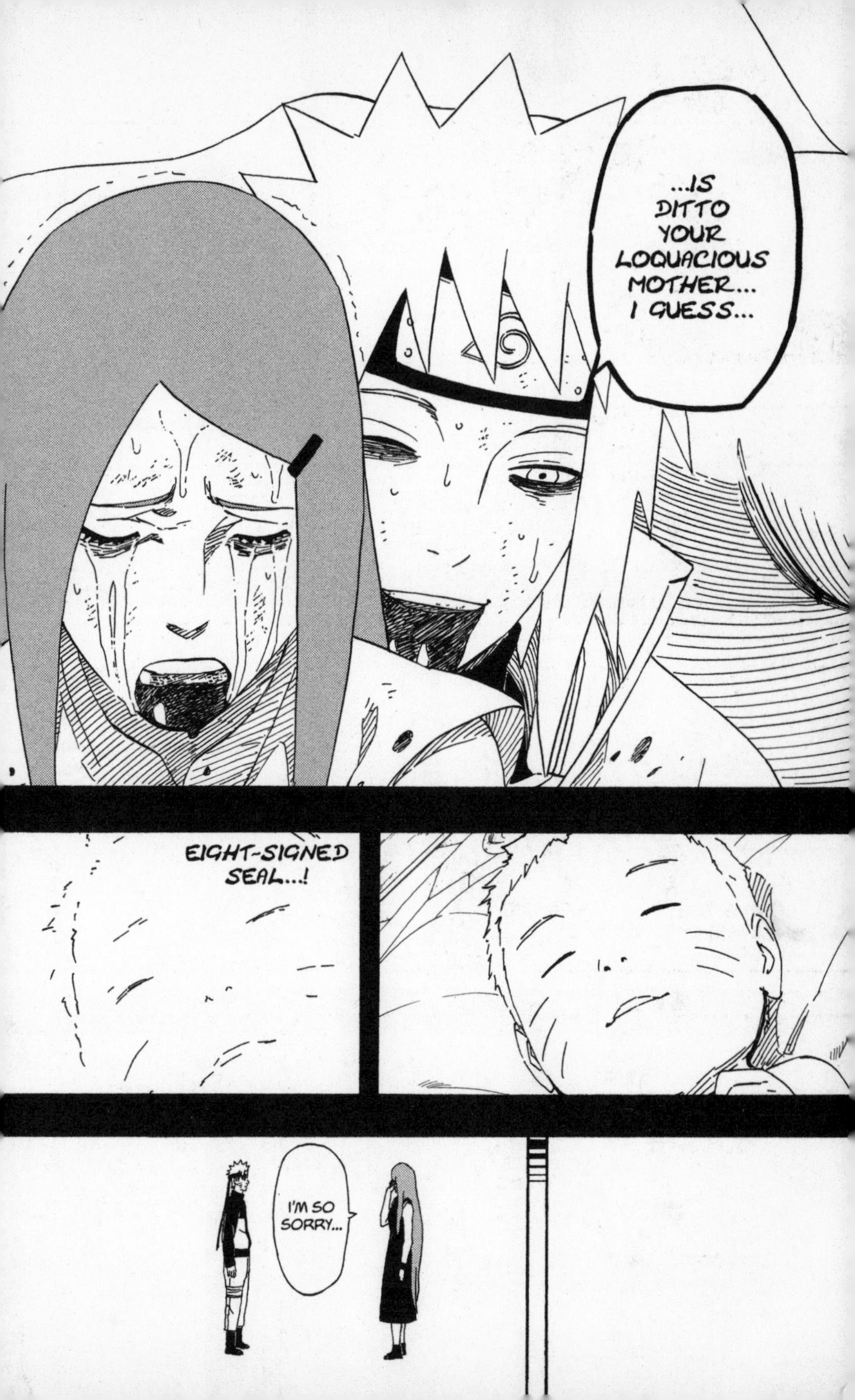
...IS DITTO YOUR LOQUACIOUS MOTHER... I GUESS...
EIGHT-SIGNED SEAL...!
I'M SO SORRY...

READ THIS WAY

...NOW I KNOW YOU ALWAYS LOVED ME!
I'M HAPPY!!

I'M GLAD I'M YOUR KID!!
FSSSH
SSH...
MINATO... ARE YOU LISTEN-ING...?!
OUR HOPES... DID REACH OUR BOY...!!
NARUTO...
!
THANK YOU FOR LETTING ME BECOME A MOTHER... AND MINATO A FATHER...
THANK YOU SO MUCH...
SHOOO...
...FOR HAVING BEEN BORN TO US!!
SWOO...
TO BE CONTINUED IN NARUTO VOLUME 54!

IN THE NEXT VOLUME...

PEACE VIADUCT

Naruto and his team engage in an intense battle with the Akatsuki organization as both sides seek the power to determine the future of their land. Internecine fighting weakens the Akatsuki, but will their power sideline Naruto?

AVAILABLE MARCH 2012!
READ IT FIRST IN SHONEN JUMP MAGAZINE!

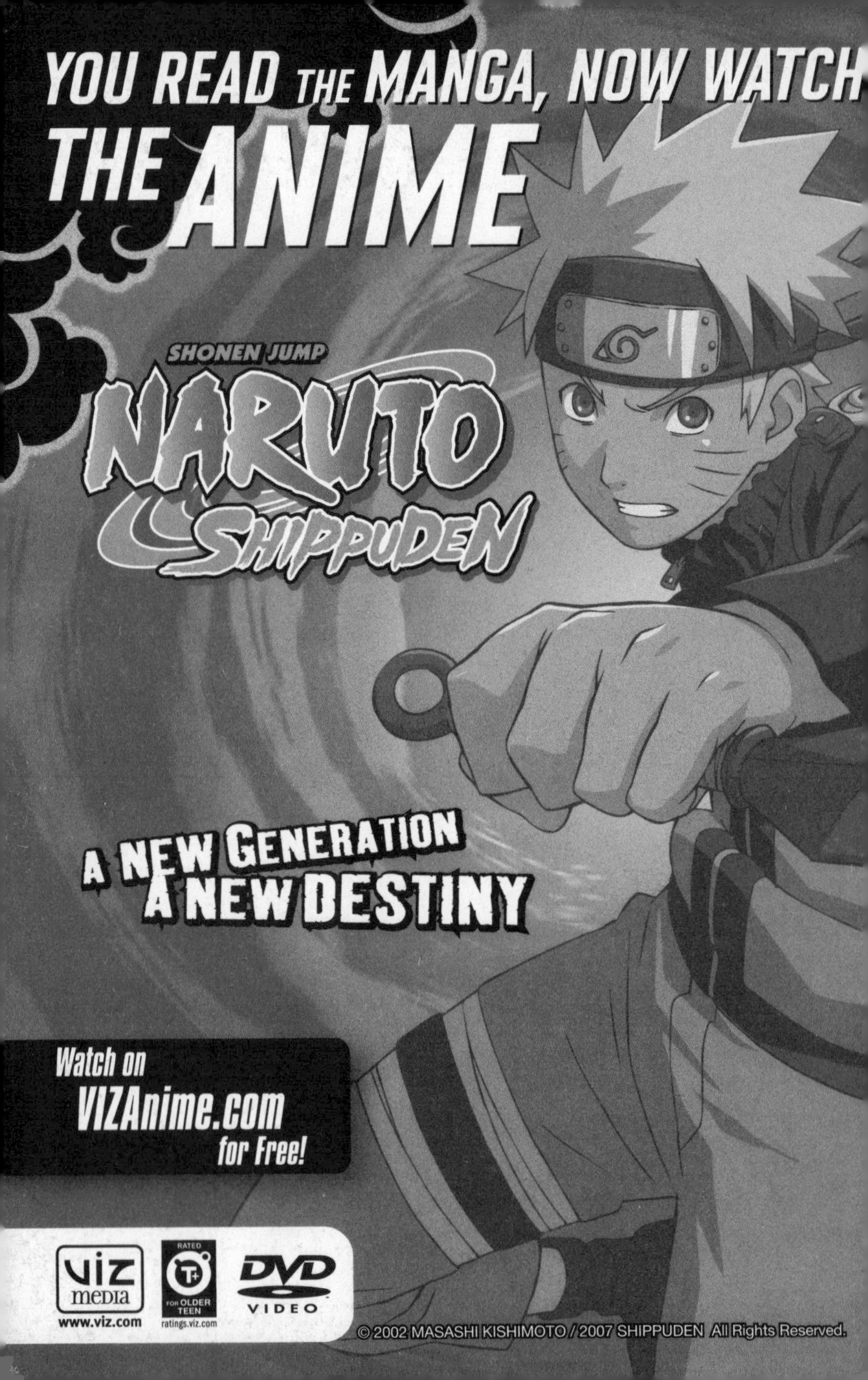
YOU READ THE MANGA, NOW WATCH
THE ANIME
SHONEN JUMP
NARUTO
SHIPPUDEN
A NEW GENERATION
A NEW DESTINY
Watch on
VIZAnime.com
for Free!
viz media
www.viz.com
RATED
T+
FOR OLDER TEEN
ratings.viz.com
DVD VIDEO
© 2002 MASASHI KISHIMOTO / 2007 SHIPPUDEN All Rights Reserved.

SHONEN JUMP
NARUTO
THE MOVIE SHIPPUDEN
-Bonds- 絆